Animals - General

Invertebrates

WHAT IS AN ANIMAL?

Ted O'Hare

Rourke

Publishing LLC
Vero Beach, Florida 32964

www.rourkepublishing.com

PHOTO CREDITS: All photos ©Lynn M. Stone except p.11 ©Marty Snyderman.

Title page: The monarch butterfly's amazing migration may take it from northern states to mountains near Mexico City.

Editor: Frank Sloan

Cover and interior design by Nicola Stratford

Library of Congress Cataloging-in-Publication Data

O'Hare, Ted, 1961-
    Invertebrates / Ted O'Hare.
        p. cm. -- (What is an animal?)
    Includes bibliographical references and index.
    ISBN 1-59515-419-1 (hardcover)
    1. Invertebrates--Juvenile literature. I. Title. II. Series: O'Hare, Ted,
1961-   What is an animal?
    QL362.4.O39 2006
    592--dc22

Printed in the USA

CG/CG

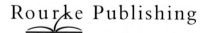
Rourke Publishing

www.rourkepublishing.com – sales@rourkepublishing.com
Post Office Box 3328, Vero Beach, FL 32964
1-800-394-7055

Table of Contents

Invertebrates

Invertebrates make up a huge group of animals that come in many kinds. Some look like small, fleshy blobs or even flowers. Others, like the octopus, have much more complicated bodies.

Invertebrates have different shapes, habits, and even body parts. But invertebrates do share one characteristic. They do not have a backbone. Invertebrates are spineless.

The lobster belongs to a phylum of invertebrate animals called crustaceans:

Invertebrate Habits

Some invertebrates, like sponges and mussels, spend their lives in one place. Boring? Sure, but not all invertebrates are stuck in the mud or on a rock in the ocean. Most kinds of insects, for example, can fly. Other invertebrates crawl, swim, walk, or float from place to place.

DiD YOU KNOW?
Scientists know of some two million kinds of invertebrates. Each has somewhat different habits from the others.

The Portuguese man-of-war's purple float allows it to sail with ocean currents that sometimes wash it ashore.

7

Kinds of Invertebrates

About 97 of every 100 kinds of animals are invertebrates. You know some of them, such as insects, spiders, clams, **sea stars**, jellyfish, worms, and crabs. Many others are known largely just to scientists.

Scientists separate animals into groups. First, animals are separated into about 30 groups called **phyla**. Only one phylum is not made up entirely of invertebrates.

The largest phylum, **arthropoda**, includes insects and spiders. Three of every four kinds of animals are arthropods.

This tarantula is a type of spider.

Where Invertebrates Live

Many kinds of insects fly. But sooner or later, even flying insects return to earth. And that's where most invertebrates spend their entire lives. They live in mud, dirt or sand, on plants, and in streams, lakes, and oceans. A very few even live on the frozen continent of Antarctica. They also live in buildings!

Some **coral** animals make their own buildings—tubes of rocky **limestone**.

A tropical fish swims among colorful coral "branches."

Mollusks, like this snail, make up the largest group of ocean animals.

The crustacean group, which includes shrimp and crabs, make up the second largest group of ocean animals.

Invertebrate Bodies

Some invertebrates are so small that they can be seen only with a microscope. Most invertebrates, however, from ticks to worms, spiders, and squid, can be seen easily.

Invertebrates have soft, boneless bodies. But many have shells of one kind or another.

Invertebrates like jellyfish and sponges have very simple body plans. They have few body **organs**.

DID YOU KNOW?

Other invertebrates, such as the lobster and squid, have many body parts. They have fairly good eyesight and the means to move about quickly.

This extremely rare giant squid is preserved in a display at Mote Marine Labratory in Sarasota, Florida.

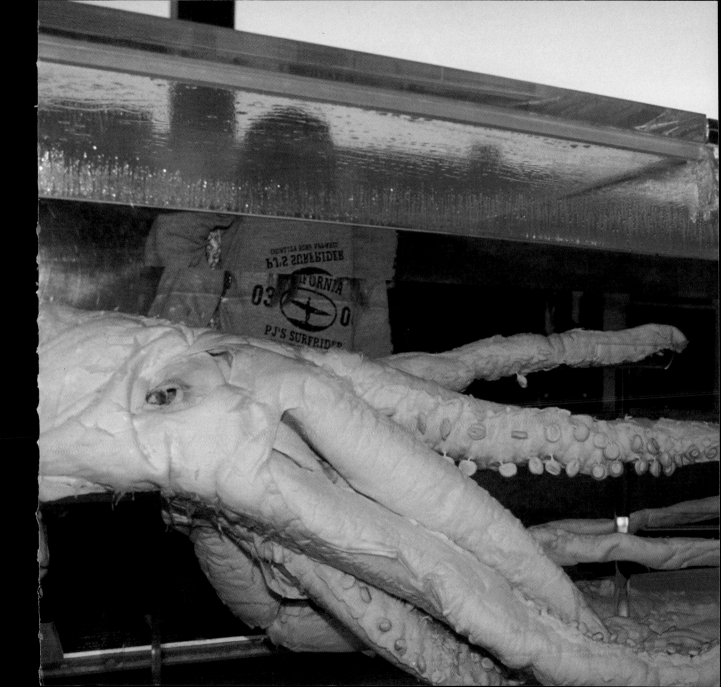

Amazing Invertebrates

We humans find some of the ways invertebrates survive quite amazing. The sea hare, for example, can squirt "ink" into the water to scare off other animals. Sea anemones and jellyfish catch food and defend themselves with stingers.

Monarch butterflies fly many hundreds of miles from the United States to a winter home in Mexico.

DiD YOU KNOW?
The cicada lives underground for 17 years before popping out.

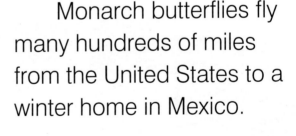

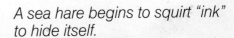

A sea hare begins to squirt "ink" to hide itself.

Predator and Prey

Animals spend much of their lives as predator, prey, or both. Predators are hunters. They eat other animals, called their prey.

Sea stars, crabs, certain snails, and dragonflies are among the best known invertebrate predators. Mostly, they prey upon other invertebrates. Sea stars, for example, attack oysters and clams.

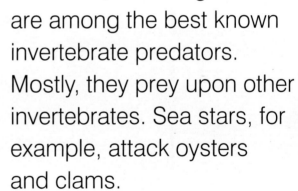

DID YOU KNOW?

As predators, crabs eat animals they catch. But crabs and many other invertebrates are often prey for larger animals, like birds and whales.

A heron is a bigger, quicker predator than the blue crab it has caught.

Baby Invertebrates

Invertebrate babies may look like tiny samples of their parents. But many others hatch from eggs and become adults through a series of stages called **metamorphosis**.

Insect metamorphosis is well known. Among many insects, the stages include egg, **larva**, and adult. In the larva stage, the insect still looks nothing like its parents. A caterpillar, for instance, is the larva stage of a moth or butterfly.

This caterpillar is the larva stage of a polyphemus moth.

People and Invertebrates

We find some invertebrates useful, like the silkworm for its silk. We find others dangerous. Certain jellyfish stingers can injure or even kill. Some mosquitoes carry disease.

We find shrimp and lobster tasty. We find termites troublesome. They eat wood.

We also count some invertebrates, such as butterflies and sea anemones, among nature's great beauties.

GLOSSARY

arthropoda (AR thre POD uh) — a phyla of invertebrate animals including insects and spiders

coral (KOR ul) — small, soft ocean invertebrates, some of which produce limestone tubes that form huge, rocky shelves called reefs

larva (LAR vuh) — an early stage of growth for certain kinds of animals and in which an animal looks and acts differently than the adults of its kind

limestone (LYME STON) — a rock-hard substance made from a liquid produced in the bodies of certain ocean animals, such as corals

metamorphosis (MET uh MOR fuh sus) — a series of changes that happen as certain animals become adults by going through stages

organs (OR gunz) — the important parts of an animal's life support system, such as its heart or digestion system

phyla (FYE luh) — direct lines of descent within a group; plural of phylum

sea stars (SEE STARZ) — a group of ocean invertebrates with "arms" or rays that spread from the sea star's center; sometimes called "starfish"

Index

Further Reading

Ball, Jacqueline A. *Invertebrates*. Gareth Stevens, 2002
Galko, Francine. *Invertebrates*. Heinemann Library, 2003
Pascoe, Elaine. *Animals without Backbones*. Powerkids Press, 2003

Websites to Visit

http://www.kidport.com/RefLib/Science/Animals/AnimalIndexInv.htm
http://www.biologybrowser.org

About the Author

Ted O'Hare is an author and editor of children's books. He divides his time between New York City and a home upstate.